MAKE THE Team

DISCARD

SOCCER

A heads-up guide to super soccer!

Richard J. Brenner

A *Sports Illustrated For Kids* Book

First Edition

Library of Congress Cataloging-in-Publication Data

Brenner, Richard J., 1941–
    Make the team, soccer—a heads up guide to super soccer / by Richard Brenner.—1st ed.
       p.   cm.
    "A Sports illustrated for kids book."
    Summary: Instructions for improving soccer skills. Discusses dribbling, heading, playmaking, defense, conditioning, mental attitude, how to handle problems with coaches, parents, and other players, and the history of soccer.
    ISBN 0-316-10751-4(hc)
    ISBN 0-316-10750-6(pb)
    1. Soccer—Juvenile literature.   [1. Soccer.]   I. Title.
II. Title: Heads up guide to super soccer.
GV943.25.B74   1990
796.334'2—dc20   89-48230
                                                 CIP
                                                   AC

SPORTS ILLUSTRATED FOR KIDS is a trademark of
THE TIME INC. MAGAZINE COMPANY.

Sports Illustrated For Kids Books is a joint imprint of Little, Brown and Company and Warner Juvenile Books. This title is published in arrangement with Cloverdale Press Inc.

10 9 8 7 6 5 4 3 2 1

BP

For further information regarding this title, write to
Little, Brown and Company, 34 Beacon Street, Boston, MA 02108.

Published simultaneously in Canada
by Little, Brown & Company (Canada) Limited

Printed in the United States of America

For my son, Jason,
my all-time favorite soccer star;
for my daughter, Halle,
who was always there, always offering encouragement;
for my wife, Anita,
for her help;
and for all my boys on the Braves,
Tacklers and Dragons,
thanks for all the fun!

CONTENTS

Chapter 1

The Most Popular Sport in the World

*T*he roots of soccer can be traced back more than 2,000 years and to countries as diverse as China, Greece and Rome. The Chinese played a game that they called *tsu chu* (meaning "to kick the ball with the feet"). They used a leather ball, and had goal posts that were 30 feet high—as high as a house!

The ancient Romans played a version of the game, which they called *harpastum*. When in the first century B.C., the Romans conquered the land we now call England, they brought their game along. It was in England that the game would evolve into its present form, and from there it spread throughout the world.

In 11th-century England two entire villages would play against each other. As many as 500 people would be on each team! A game would begin at the mid-point between the two villages, and it wouldn't end until one of the teams kicked an object—originally a human skull and later the inflated bladder of an animal—to the center of the opposing village.

The contests were played without rules and resembled riots more than they did games. Violence was common. Still, the matches became extremely popular. They were *so* popular that some English kings found it necessary to ban them! They felt that too many people were getting injured. Also, this new sport was taking away from time spent practicing archery, a skill necessary for defending the nation.

It wasn't until 1848 that official rules of play were established. The game was called football then, and in 1863 a group of players met and formed the Football Association.

The word "soccer" came about when people in England shortened the word "association" to "soc" and added a few letters.

This was during the period when England was the world's most powerful nation, with ships that sailed all over the globe. English sailors and settlers spread the game wherever they went, and soccer quickly became the most popular sport in the world.

In most of the world today the game is still known by each country's equivalent of the word "football." If you happen to be in Germany, for instance, you play *fussball*, while in Spain and South America they play *futbol*. In England, the game is called football.

In 1904 an international organization was founded in Zurich, Switzerland, to establish one set of rules and to govern the sport. It is called the Federation Internationale de Football Associats, or FIFA for short. FIFA also oversees the World Cup, the most widely contested of all sports championships.

The World Cup tournament is played every four years and draws all-star teams from close to 150 countries. Those teams compete to become one of the 24 finalists. Those 24 teams then gather in one country to compete for the honor of becoming the reigning king of soccer. More than a billion fans from around the world tune in their radios or TV sets to the World Cup championship game.

In the United States soccer has never been as popular as some other sports, such as baseball, basketball and American football. During the 1970s the North American Soccer League (NASL), which had 24 teams, went all out to establish professional soccer as a major sport in the United States. Teams imported some of the world's best players to increase the level of competition. The New York Cosmos even signed Pele, the forward from Brazil who is still considered to be the greatest soccer player of all time. Pele did his part, leading the Cosmos to the 1977 NASL Championship in front of 77,690 cheering fans at Giants Stadium in New Jersey. Soon after this peak, however, the popularity of professional soccer declined, and the league was disbanded.

But don't count soccer out! In 1990, the United States national team played in the World Cup finals, which was held in Italy. It was the first time in 40 years a U.S. team made the finals! Now interest in soccer in America is increasing. In 1994, the United States will be the host country for the World Cup. This means an automatic berth for the U.S. team. It also means that soccer fans all over the world will be focusing their attention on the United States.

By the way, soccer may not be a big spectator sport in the United States, but that doesn't mean it's not popular. Did you know that more young people in the United States play soccer than play Little League baseball? Soccer may never be as popular in this country as baseball, basketball or football, but it is a great game that is fun to play and watch.

About This Book

Make The Team: Soccer has been designed as a complete course in the game. Whether you're just getting started or have played a bit and want to improve, you'll find what you need in the pages to follow.

Before you turn to the actual skills and drills that make up the bulk of this book, be sure to read the overview of the game that explains the rules, the players' roles and a variety of other basics. This will give you what you need to get started.

After you've been through the skills and drills, you'll want to read the chapter called "Putting It All Together" for explanations of the basic strategies and tactics you'll need to know when game time arrives.

Throughout *Make The Team: Soccer* you'll find special boxes devoted to particular problems you may face while playing and learning to play soccer.

It's important to remember that, although you'll be reading this book as an individual who wants to play heads-up soccer, soccer is a team sport. You never can become as good a player as Pele, if you aren't a team player. That's the beauty of the game at any level—from World Cup to pick-up games.

Now, let's talk soccer!

Chapter 2

EQUIPMENT

When it comes to playing soccer, you need a few basic pieces of equipment and a few basic exercises to get your body in shape. You might consider asking your parents to help pay for some of the gear. It costs about $65 to buy a ball, good shoes, shin guards and a water container. If you think you or your parents might have trouble raising the money—and $65 *is* a lot of money— talk to your coach or local youth league counselor to see if there are other options. Sometimes, for instance, local businesses such as shops or banks sponsor teams and even stake them to full uniforms. Hand-me-down or second-hand shoes—as long as they fit well—are another possibility.

Balls

It is very helpful if each player has his or her own ball. Having your own ball allows you to practice on your own in your school yard or in a park, with or without friends. In addition, at team practices almost all the training exercises are done with a ball. If there aren't enough balls to go around, there can be a lot of standing around and not very much gets done.

Soccer balls are made of different materials, and their cost ($10–$15) varies depending upon what material is selected and whether or not a professional player's name is printed on the ball. A plain rubber waterproof inflatable ball is all you really need for practice. Having a famous player's name on the ball doesn't make it any better.

Soccer balls come in different sizes. The sizes are numbered from 3 to 5. Players from ages 6 to 11 usually use a No. 4 ball. Players 12 and over use a No. 5 ball, which is slightly larger and somewhat heavier. Try always to practice with the same size ball that you play with in a game. Remember also to keep your ball inflated properly, following the guidelines printed right on the ball.

Shoes

Soccer is a game that requires constant movement, and it's difficult to run or kick a ball when you're not wearing the proper shoes. Because you are going to be running a lot and moving your feet in many different ways, your shoe should be both lightweight and flexible. A good shoe has padding to protect your Achilles tendon—which connects the muscles in your calf to the bone of your heel—and to cushion the heel and arch. Your shoes should also have rubber cleats on the bottom to provide the traction you will need to run and make sharp pivots. A good pair of shoes should cost about $40.

Here are some hints about shoe shopping:

● Shop toward the end of the day. Feet tend to swell a bit as the day goes on. Shoes that feel fine in the store in the morning may feel uncomfortably snug in the afternoon.

● When you try on shoes, wear the same type of socks in which you play and practice.

● Don't be shy about running or practicing certain soccer moves while you're in the shoe store. (This doesn't mean you should bring your ball along!) Simply standing or sitting with a new pair of shoes on your feet will not give you a sense of how they will feel on the field. You may have to put up with some strange looks from other shoppers, however!

Socks

There's no big decision here. Whatever kind you're comfortable with is fine, whether cotton or nylon.

Shin Guards

Some people think shin guards should be a required part of the soccer uniform. Though there are no actual rules about this, every player should wear shin guards in all practices and games. They offer valuable protection from stray kicks.

Shin guards are available in many styles and materials, and cost roughly $10–$12 a pair. Two kinds are most popular: plastic-cased shin guards that are worn under the sock, and shin guards that have the protective material built right into the sock.

Goalkeeper's Equipment

Goalies need what everybody else needs, and then some. Because they spend a lot of time diving on the ground and leaping into the air to make saves, as well as having run-ins with other players anxious to score goals, they need some special equipment.

Because goalies frequently land on their elbows, collide with other players and run the risk of getting kicked in the head or groin, anyone who plays goalie should, at a minimum, wear knee pads ($5-$6), elbow pads ($5-$6) and a helmet ($15). If you play in a league that doesn't require goalies to wear a helmet, and the team doesn't have a regular goalie, it might be a good idea for everyone to chip in to buy a team helmet. Male goalies should wear a plastic protective cup and athletic supporter.

Optional pieces of equipment for goalies include:

- Sliding pads to protect the hips, back and chest.

- A long-sleeved shirt and long pants (when it's not too hot) to avoid scrapes.

- Gloves—Some goalies think gloves improve their grip on the ball; others like to feel the ball on their fingers. Gloves are recommended in cold weather to keep the hands from stiffening up.

A goalie always has to wear a shirt that is of a different color from that of the jerseys worn by his or her teammates. This is so the attacking team knows who the goalkeeper is.

A Portable Drinking Container

A portable drinking container should also be considered a piece of basic equipment. The plastic type with a built-in straw is preferable and costs about $3. It is extremely important that you take breaks regularly during practice and as often as you can during a game to drink some juice or water. While you're running and perspiring, your body is losing liquids; these liquids need to be replaced if you are to avoid muscle cramps and heat exhaustion.

Chapter 3

The Warm-Up

All the gear in the world won't help you if your body isn't in shape to begin with—and warmed up before every practice and game. Here are some basic steps to take to get your body going.

Warming Up

Warming up for a few minutes before a practice or game is good preparation for both your mind and your body. Warming up sends your brain a wake-up signal and gets your body ready for strenuous exercise. It's also a good way to avoid pulling a muscle, which can happen easily if you exert yourself suddenly. A good way to start your warm-up is with a series of stretching exercises.

● To stretch the *hamstring* muscle, which is the long muscle that runs from the back of your knee to the buttocks, try this exercise:

1. Holding on to a bench, a fence or a friend, lift one foot off the ground and bend your leg at the knee.

2. Grab your foot and hold it against your backside for a count of 10.

3. Switch legs and repeat the stretch.

4. Repeat three times with each leg.

Eventually you'll be able to do this without holding on to anything.

● To stretch your *groin* muscle, which is the muscle in the fold between the lower part of your body and your upper thigh:

1. *Sit on the floor or ground.*

2. *Put the soles of your feet together, and pull them toward you while holding your knees on or close to the ground.*

3. *Grasping your ankles, hold that position for a count of 10.*

4. *Relax and repeat three times.*

● To stretch your *calf* muscle:

1. *Get in a push-up position, but put one knee on the ground.*

2. *Put your weight on the toes of your other foot, and then push the heel down until you feel a slight pull.*

3. *Hold that position for a count of 10.*

4. *Switch legs and repeat the stretch.*

5. *Repeat three times with each leg.*

● To stretch your *back* muscles:

1. *Lying on your back, raise one leg and, grabbing the leg right below the knee, slowly bring it up to your chest.*

2. *Keeping your other leg straight and your head on the ground, hold this position for a count of 10.*

3. *Switch legs and repeat the stretch.*

4. *Repeat three times with each leg.*

● To stretch your *shoulders:*

1. *Move one arm across your body, almost as if you were going to take a backhand swing.*

2. *Grasp the elbow of the arm in motion with your other hand and gently pull the arm further across your body.*

3. Gently pull the elbow toward you for a count of 10.
4. Switch arms and repeat the stretch.
5. Repeat three times with each arm.

Now that you are stretched, you should do a *general warm-up*, such as jogging lightly or running in place for a few minutes. Remember, you're not trying to break any speed records or use up your energy before you take the field.

After you've completed the general warm-up, you should work on the techniques that you use during a game. (In the following chapters, you'll find drills that will help you do this.)

There might be some people on your team who don't understand the value of warm-ups and think they're a waste of time. If you have any doubts about the importance of warming-up and stretching, just ask yourself why all professional teams, who have done a lot of exercise research, insist that their players warm up before they play or practice. This is how champions are made and kept healthy!

You Are What You Eat

Make sure you eat a balanced diet from the four basic food groups: dairy, meat, grains, and fruits and vegetables. Don't eat too much food that is high in calories and low in nutrition—yes, we mean french fries, candy and potato chips. Think of it this way: You are what you eat, and you don't want to be junk.

Staying In Shape

Part of being in shape means eating well. Another factor is getting enough sleep. Even a finely tuned engine needs some rest. The third ingredient is following a regular exercise routine. *Don't begin any exercise program without first consulting your parents or guardian and someone, such as a gym teacher, who is knowledgeable about training programs. Working closely with people who know will guarantee that you come up with the program that's best for you.*

If you regularly practice the soccer drills in this book you will be well on your way toward getting yourself in tip-top shape. If you want to get in even better shape, though, you can add a running program and calisthenics, such as chin-ups and sit-ups. The best type of running program for soccer players is to alternate long runs—30 to 40 yards—with short bursts of 10 yards. That way you imitate real game conditions while improving your stamina and quickness.

Keep in mind that every time you play a soccer game you are going to run hundreds, sometimes even thousands, of yards. That's going to require a lot of stamina, especially near the end of the game. Lots of games are won and lost in the last few minutes, and it's almost always the team whose athletes are in better condition that wins.

Chapter 4

A Bird's-Eye View

Before we start talking about the actual skills and drills needed to play soccer, it's extremely important that you have a good overview of the game. That means understanding how all the various parts of the game—the rules, the players—work together. Let's start with . . .

The Playing Field

A soccer field is a rectangle. An official-size field used by professionals may be anywhere between 100 and 130 yards long and 50 to 100 yards wide. Youth leagues play on much smaller fields. Regardless of their size, all soccer fields are laid out exactly the same way (see the diagram on page 29).

The long sides of the rectangle are called *touchlines* or *sidelines*. The shorter sides are called the *goal lines* or *endlines*. A *halfway line* or *midfield line* divides the field in half.

The vertical poles of the goal are called *goalposts*, and the horizontal piece is called a *crossbar*. To score a goal the ball must pass completely over the endline, between the goalposts and under the crossbar.

The *goal area* is a rectangle located directly in front of each goal. This is the area from which goal kicks (see chapter 5) are taken. A goal kick is awarded to the team defending the goal when the attacking team kicks the ball out of bounds past the endline. (You'll learn more about this later.) The *penalty area* is a rectangle that is drawn around each goal area. Within these two areas, goalies are allowed to touch the ball with their hands.

The *penalty spot* is located in the penalty area. This is

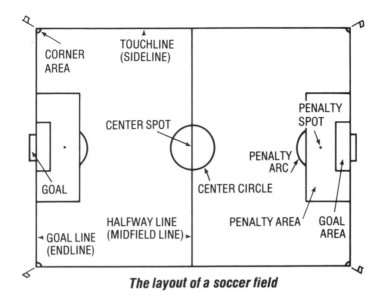

The layout of a soccer field

the spot from which penalty shots are taken (penalty shots are explained in chapter 5). The *penalty arc* is a semicircle that is drawn outside of the center of the penalty area. It has a radius of 10 yards from the penalty spot and serves as a reminder to players that they must be 10 yards away from a player who is taking a penalty shot.

The *corner area* is a small arc that is drawn at each of the four corners of the field. When the defending team kicks or knocks the ball past its own endline, the attacking team is awarded a corner kick from within the corner area.

The *center circle* is located in the middle of the field. It has a radius of 10 yards from the *center spot*, which is the exact center of the field. All kickoffs are taken at the center spot.

Length of Game

An official adult game takes 90 minutes and is played in two 45-minute halves or periods, with a 5-minute rest period between the two halves. Youth leagues may play shorter halves. The final whistle ends most games, even if the score is tied.

But if the teams are playing a championship match, the game goes into overtime. In an official FIFA game the overtime period consists of two 15-minute halves, with a 2-minute rest between halves. If the score is still tied after the overtime period, the teams play what is known as a *shoot-out*. In a shoot-out, five players, first from one team, then from the other team, each take one penalty kick. If one team scores more goals, it is declared the winner. If the score is still tied after the five penalty kicks, then the teams alternate taking penalty kicks, one per team, until there is a winner. Both teams must take the same number of kicks before a winner is declared.

The Lineup

A soccer team fields 11 players, one of whom is a goalie. The other 10 players play positions that can be divided generally into three main groups.

1. Fullbacks. A fullback's major responsibility is to play defense in his team's goal area.

2. Midfielders. Midfielders have a dual role. They assist the fullbacks when the ball is in their defensive zone, and they help the forwards create scoring opportunities in the attacking zone.

3. Forwards. The primary role of a forward is to score goals. Forwards play most of the game in the attacking zone around their opponents' goal.

The goalkeeper's main role is to stop the other team from scoring. Not surprisingly, a goalie spends most of the game in his team's penalty area.

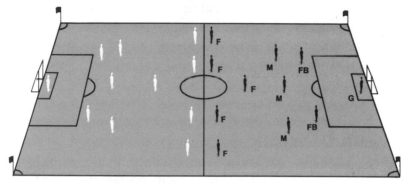

These teams are lined up in 2-3-5 formation (FB stands for fullback, M for midfielder, F for forward and G for goalkeeper)

Formations

The way a coach positions the players is known as a *formation*. Formations can be designated by the number of players assigned to each of the basic positions. For example, if a coach told the players to line up in a 4–3–3 formation, they would know that he wanted a lineup with four fullbacks, three midfielders and three forwards. If the coach wanted to put more emphasis on attack, he would order a 3–3–4 lineup, which would put four players at forward, or even a 2–3–5, which would put five players up front.

31

The formation a coach selects is based on three considerations:

• The philosophy of the coach: Does he or she prefer an offensive or defensive style of play?

• The skills of the players: Does the coach have an abundance of good forwards, or players who would be better used as fullbacks and midfielders?

• The game situation: For example if a team is ahead 3–1 late in the game, the coach may decide to protect the lead by using more fullbacks and midfielders and fewer forwards.

Substitutions

FIFA regulations allow a coach to select up to five players per game from which to choose substitutes. But only two of the five may actually be used in a game. A player who has been replaced by a substitute may not return to the game.

Youth leagues establish their own rules regarding substitutions. It is very common for teams to play with unlimited substitutions, which means that a coach may send players into and out of the game at any time.

The Game Officials

There are usually three officials assigned to a game—a *referee* and two *linespeople*. The referee is responsible for enforcing the 17 laws, or rules, of soccer and is given absolute authority to do so. Using a whistle to start and stop play, and hand signals to communicate calls, the referee is in complete charge of the field and the players.

The referee calls all penalties and when necessary warns or ejects players. The referee may also decide to ignore a penalty if he or she decides that calling it would give an advantage to the team that broke the rule. For example, if a player was fouled while attempting to go around an opponent, but was still able to break away, the referee could decide that stopping play would actually penalize the team that had been fouled.

If a player is injured, the referee decides whether the injury is serious enough to stop play. The referee is also the official timekeeper, and can cancel a game because of bad weather.

The linespeople are stationed on each sideline. Subject to the decision of the referee, they use flags to indicate when a ball is out of play, and which team is entitled to the corner kick, goal kick or throw-in. The linespeople also assist the referee by pointing out violations that the referee might have missed. But in all cases the final decision is made by the referee.

Violations, Misconduct and Penalties

The laws of soccer divide violations, or fouls, into two groups: major and minor. If the referee judges the violations to be intentional, he will rule it a major violation. These are the major violations:

1. *Kicking or attempting to kick a player.*
2. *Tripping an opponent.*
3. *Leaping through the air to tackle or block.*

4. Running at or into an opponent in a dangerous manner.

5. Charging an opponent from behind unless the opponent is obstructing the ball.

6. Striking or attempting to strike an opponent.

7. Holding an opponent.

8. Pushing an opponent.

9. Touching the ball with a hand or arm (except for goalies who are inside their own penalty areas).

When a major violation is committed, the referee awards a direct free kick to the team that was fouled. The kick is taken at the spot on the field at which the foul occurred. A direct free kick is one on which a goal can be scored.

If a major violation is committed by the defensive team within its own penalty area—in other words, near the goal that team is defending—the referee awards the attacking team a penalty kick. (Penalty kicks are discussed in more detail in the next chapter.) It doesn't matter whether the *ball* is in the penalty area when the foul occurs. As long as the *foul* takes place in the penalty area, a penalty kick is granted.

If the referee judges a violation to be unintentional, he will rule it a *minor violation* and award an *indirect free kick* at the spot at which the violation was committed. Unlike a direct free kick, an indirect free kick must be touched by at least one other player before a goal can be scored. These are the minor violations:

1. Playing in a reckless or dangerous manner—for instance, trying to kick the ball while it is being held by the goalkeeper.

2. Illegally charging or running at a player, which means, either charging a player who does not have the ball, or charging a player who does have the ball but charging from too great a distance.

3. Keeping an opponent from going after the ball when you yourself do not have it.

4. Charging the goalkeeper in the goal area, except when the goalkeeper is holding the ball or obstructing an opponent.

5. Misplaying or stalling by the goalie. The goalie may not take more than four steps before kicking or throwing the ball to another player. In addition, the goalie may not simply hold onto the ball to delay the game.

In addition to calling fouls, the referee also issues *cautions* to offending players in certain situations. A caution is a warning to the player; the referee signals a caution by holding up a yellow card. Here are reasons for a caution:

1. A player enters the field to join or rejoin his team after the game has begun without first receiving permission from the referee.

2. A player repeatedly violates the rules of the game.

3. A player argues or in any way (such as kicking at the ground) disagrees with a referee's decision.

4. A player behaves in an unsportsmanlike manner.

In the last three cases, the referee will also award an indirect free kick. A player who receives two yellow cards will be ejected from the game. The referee will also eject a player who fights, uses bad language or who, in the opinion of the referee, intentionally breaks the rules. No substitutions are permitted for ejected players. Therefore, when a player is ejected from a game, the entire team is penalized because they must play with fewer players than the other team.

Each player should always play soccer cleanly, fairly and with respect for opponents and officials. There is absolutely no reason to foul an opponent intentionally or to abuse or question an official. You not only discredit yourself; you also hurt your team.

The Offside Rule

The Offside Rule was adopted to stop forwards from "hanging" at the goal, waiting to receive long passes and turn them into easy scores.

To put this complex rule as simply as possible: You cannot be ahead of the ball in the *attacking zone*—from the midfield line to your opponent's goal—when it is kicked

?

■ *WHAT IF* somebody on the other team is playing dirty and getting away with it?

If an opponent is playing dirty, the worst thing you can do is retaliate. You don't want to bring yourself down to the same low level as your opponent. Instead, ask the referee in a polite way to keep an eye on the player. If that doesn't work, ask your coach to talk to the other team's coach. The important thing is not to let the dirty tactics distract you. Keep playing the game the way it was meant to be played, by the rules.

there by a teammate, unless there are two members of the other team (the defenders) between you and the goal. Every good rule has exceptions, and in this case you can be ahead of the ball if you receive the ball directly from a goal kick, a corner kick, a throw-in or when it is dropped by the referee. Remember, no one is offside until the ball is passed into the attacking zone and the referee blows the whistle.

The team whose player is called offside has to give up the ball, and the opposing team then takes an indirect free kick from the place where the ball was kicked.

The offside rule may seem a little confusing to you at first (O.K., *very* confusing), but after you've thought about it and played for a while, it will be easier to understand.

Practicing

Practicing can be fun, but it can also get pretty boring sometimes, especially when you do the same drill over and over. Try to remember that repeating the drills is the way to learn new skills. It's like playing the piano—you can't make music if you haven't practiced the scales.

Teamwork

Teamwork is the basic foundation of successful soccer. It's the magic that turns a disorganized bunch of kids into a functioning group. Sure, you need the skills to play the game, but you have to blend those skills with the skills of the other players in order to have a *team*. Even a group of all-stars wouldn't win very often if they didn't play together as a team. Just imagine a stage full of talented musicians with each one playing a different tune and ignoring the conductor. They might be great musicians, but they will never become a great orchestra until they begin to play together.

The essential principle of teamwork is that players must *always* put the good of the team ahead of any dreams of personal glory. Everyone would like to score the goal that wins the game. But if a player finds himself in position to take a pretty good shot on goal, then notices a teammate completely unguarded in front of the net, the player ought to pass the ball. The player who scores the goal, even while jumping up and down in celebration, should realize that it took a lot of work by the team to set up the shot.

Teamwork isn't only about passing the ball and helping out on defense. It's also about having a good attitude toward your teammates and coach. It's about cheering a teammate for making a good play or learning a new skill, and about offering encouragement instead of blame when a teammate makes a mistake or is having difficulty learning a skill. Teamwork also means working on your own skills, which will contribute to the overall success of the team. Showing up on time for practices and games is also a sign of teamwork; it shows cooperation and caring, two basics for successful teamwork.

Your Coach

Coaches are the men and women who must take the players—you and your teammates—and try to create a winning squad. They have to figure out who works best at each position, help everyone improve their skills at each position and then show the individual players how to function as a team. They have to get along with their players—and discipline them when things go wrong. They have to keep up a team's spirits after losses—for even good coaches have losing seasons. What a job!

Coaches come in all shapes and sizes, and have different levels of ability—just like players. Your coach may have a lot or only a small amount of knowledge about soccer and how to teach skills or coach a team. Coaches also come with different personalities, with some more friendly and understanding than others.

Chances are that your coach likes kids and sports. As long as your coach is fair and not abusive, respect the fact that he is giving time to the team and doing the best job of coaching that he or she knows how to do.

One way you can show respect is to show up on time for all games and practices. If you can't make a game or a practice, let the coach know as far in advance as possible. Another way to show respect is to listen when your coach talks, and to save the horsing around for after practice.

Sometimes a coach and a player have different ideas about which position a player is best suited for. It's all right to ask the coach to let you try a new position, but timing can be key. Don't bring it up during a game or in the middle of practice, when a coach has other things to think about and deal with. After all, you wouldn't like it if your brother or sister ran up to you and asked about next week's game in the middle of this week's practice, would you? Part of being on a team means you have to be willing to accept the coach's decision without kicking up a fuss, even though you may not agree with it. It may not be the right decision, but the coach makes the call—it's his job. Arguing about decisions can easily disturb the team's sense of togetherness.

You should also try to understand that the coach may not always be able to give you the attention you need or want. There may be 15 players on a team and only one coach. Remember, the coach is also a part of the team and

? _HOW DO_ I tell my parents I don't want them around when I'm playing? How do I tell them I wish they'd come and watch for a change?

Problems with parents usually involve how much attention they pay to your playing. Some parents don't come to watch any games at all, while others don't miss a single one, and run up and down the sidelines screaming instructions.

Everybody likes to have support, but remember, _you_ signed up to play, not your folks. If they're busy or tired or simply not interested in soccer, it doesn't mean they don't care about you. You're not interested in everything your parents do, either. Make sure you tell them that you'd like it if they would come. Maybe they have held back because they've been afraid you'd be embarrassed or nervous.

If, on the other hand, your parents make a nuisance of themselves whenever you play, ask them to hold their comments and suggestions until after the game. If necessary, gently remind your folks that you're playing for _you_, not for them.

like all team members needs and deserves your cooperation.

Playing for Fun

There are lots of reasons to play soccer. The first and most important is that you enjoy the game. You shouldn't play soccer because someone else wants you to, and you shouldn't play soccer if you prefer to play individual sports. There are a lot of other sports or activities—from playing the piano to tossing a football or hitting a baseball—that you might like better. But if you like running, kicking and working together with other players to form a team, and if you are willing to practice, then soccer is the game for you!

Chapter 5

THE PLAYERS

Now let's find out about the individual players who make up a soccer team.

The Goalkeeper

The goalkeeper is the only player on the field who is allowed to touch the ball with his hands and arms—*within the penalty area only*. When the goalie roams outside of the area, he is not allowed to use his hands.

Goalkeepers have both defensive and offensive roles. The goalie's major responsibility is to keep the ball out of the net. Thus a goalie has to be skilled in catching the ball or knocking it away when he can't catch it. The goalie launches the team's attack as soon as a save is made, by throwing or punting the ball back into play.

A good goalie has many different skills and can think and act quickly. Let's look more closely at the many elements there are to playing goalie.

The Basic Stance

- Your feet should be pointed slightly outward, shoulder-width apart.
- Your knees and back should be slightly bent.
- Your hands should be raised chest high.
- Your elbows should be tucked in close to your body.

Every move that a goalie makes should start from this ready position. You should assume the basic goalie stance whenever the other team is within *shooting distance*. It is basically up to the goalie to determine when the opposing team is in position to get off a shot on goal.

The goalkeeper's basic stance

The correct position of the goalie's hands when catching a ball above the waist

Catching the Ball

The most important skill for a goalie to have is the ability to catch the ball. To do this right, you should always position your hands so that they are behind the ball, with your fingers spread as wide as possible. The illustration above shows you what this means. You should also try to catch the ball with your body directly behind your hands. That way, if you miss the ball, it will bounce off your body and you will still have a chance to scoop up the rebound. When you're preparing to make a save, always keep your eyes on the ball.

Balls come at a goalie from different angles and heights, so you have to be prepared to stop all of them. Here's how:

● To catch airborne balls that are *above* your waist, you should hold your hands up in front of you. Your thumbs should almost be touching and your body should be right behind your hands.

The correct position for bringing a ground ball under control

• To catch an airborne ball *below* your waist, your fingers should point down and your little fingers should almost touch. Your legs should be positioned behind your hands as a second barrier.

• To catch a *ground ball*, you should bring your legs close together, bend from your waist (but *not* your knees) and hold your hands just a few inches off the ground. Let the ball roll up your palms to your forearms, and then, bending your arms at the elbows, cradle the ball to your chest.

Cutting Down the Angle

Most young goalies feel more comfortable defending the goal while standing on the goal line. But to become a good goalie, you have to learn to come out of the goal in certain situations. This is called *cutting down the angle*, because it cuts down the amount of goal that is available for the attacker to shoot at. Before you practice this technique, go out on the field with somebody, and have your partner stand right in front of the goal on the goal line. You can stand anywhere within the penalty box. Notice how much room there is on either side of the goalie. Then have your partner slowly walk toward you. You'll see that as the person comes closer, there is less and less open goal for you to shoot at.

Coming out to meet a player who is charging in by himself—this is called a breakaway—not only cuts down the angle but also puts pressure on the attacker. Pressure often causes mistakes. This doesn't mean that you will always make the save when you come off the goal line, but you will have a much better chance than if you stay back.

Learning how to cut down the angle properly takes a lot of practice, calculation and confidence. You have to judge how quickly the attacker is moving, and whether there is a passing opportunity. It also helps to know which foot your opponent prefers to use when shooting.

Diving

You won't be able to make every stop while standing on your feet. You may have to dive for some shots. Diving is a difficult thing to do, and you can get hurt unless you know the right way to do it. Before you practice diving, it might be a good idea to work with a knowledgeable coach.

Here's how to execute a good dive:

1. Starting from the basic stance, shift your weight to the leg closest to the ball.

2. Turn your body toward the ball.

3. Push off on the leg closest to the ball. Both arms should be stretched out. The lower hand should be

The goalkeeper's dive

directly in the path of the ball and the upper hand should move toward the top of the ball. The thumbs should almost be touching.

4. As soon as you catch the ball, protect it by curling up your body around it.

The best way to start practicing diving saves is without a ball and down on your knees. That way, you're closer to the ground and less likely to get hurt as you learn.

Punching and Deflecting

Sometimes you won't be able to catch the ball even if you dive for it. If you can't get close enough to catch a ball that you have dived for, try to get enough of your hand, fist or fingers on the ball to send it toward the sideline or around the post and over the end line. It's better to give the opposing team a corner kick than a goal.

Goalkeepers must challenge opposing players to keep the ball out of the net. This goalie used his fists to clear the ball.

The Penalty Shot

This is probably a goalkeeper's worst moment. There is a player ready to shoot the ball right at you, and you as goalie are not allowed to move until the kicker's foot touches the ball. When the ball is kicked correctly, it moves so fast that all you can do is guess and dive in one direction or the other. One thing you can try to do is confuse the kicker with a fake—moving your head and shoulder in one direction as the kicker approaches the ball and then diving the other way. But remember, you're not allowed to move your feet until the ball is kicked.

The Goalkeeper on Attack

As soon as goalies make a save and get the ball, they are transformed from the last line of defense into the first line of attack. Goalies can launch the offense with either their hands or their feet, but should always put the ball in play toward the sidelines and to a teammate who is open.

Throwing

There are two basic throws. The *underhand* throw is used for rolling the ball. The *overhand* throw is used to pass the ball through the air.

Kicking

When a goalie kicks the ball out of his hands, it is called a *punt*. To punt the ball properly:
  1. *Start by holding it in both hands.*
  2. *Take one step with your non-kicking foot.*

**The two basic throws:
underhand (above)
and overhand (left)**

3. *As you bring your kicking leg up, drop the ball straight down.*

4. *When you kick, your toes should be pointed down, and you should hit the ball with your instep (the top of your foot, in front of your ankle). You should be kicking the ball without raising your knee. If you bring your leg up too soon and kick the ball above the level of your knee, the ball will go straight up in the air instead of down the field. If you bring your leg up too late, you will probably kick a ball that bounces and doesn't travel very far.*

In General

Make sure that you get someone to give you a good workout in goaltending and that you spend enough time practicing throwing and punting.

In addition to all the physical skills that goalies need,

they also need strong "inner skills" to be successful at such a demanding position:

- **Courage** to stand in the way of powerfully kicked shots.
- **Concentration** to locate the ball through all the players in front of the goal.
- **Mental toughness** to give up a goal and not fall to pieces.
- **Confidence** to be able to challenge shooters and make quick decisions.

Fullbacks

Sometimes fullbacks are called "sweepers" or "stoppers." Whatever name they go by, their job is to stop their opponents from shooting at the goal. The way a fullback does this is to *mark* (soccer's term for guarding) an opponent as closely as possible.

The basic rule in marking an opponent is to keep your body between your opponent and the goal. That's true whether or not the player you are marking has the ball. When the player doesn't have the ball, you have to be alert and constantly aware of where both the player and the ball are. Whenever the ball is in your defensive zone, you should be up on the balls of your feet, in a slight crouch, ready to spring into action.

When the player you are marking doesn't have the ball, you still have a job to do; in fact, two jobs:

1. Practice ball denial: You practice ball denial when you mark your opponent closely and keep your body between your opponent and the ball. Because the ball and

Fullbacks—the last line of defense before the goalie.

the playing positions are constantly shifting, you must stay on your toes and be ready to move in any direction.

2. Cover your defensive teammates who are closer to the ball: Covering is the same as *backing up.* When the player you are marking doesn't have the ball, you have to be ready to take on the player who *does* have the ball if that player "escapes" from one of your teammates nearby.

The general rule for defenders is that the farther you are from the ball the less closely you mark your specific opponent. That way you can be free to help your teammates. For example if the attack is coming toward the right fullback and you are playing left fullback, you should slide toward the middle. Don't go too far, and don't lose sight of the player you are marking—you don't want to be out of position and have a pass wind up at the feet of the player you left unguarded. The other half of the general rule for defenders is that the closer you are to the ball, the tighter you mark your opponent.

When you mark an opponent who is dribbling the ball into your area, try to force him to the sidelines, away from the goal area. You do this by positioning your body so that your opponent can't move toward the middle without charging into you. The idea is to keep the attacker out of the *danger area*, and then either take the ball away with a *shoulder charge* or a *tackle* (tackles are discussed in Chapter 6), or force a weak shot or poor pass.

It's a big advantage to know whether your opponent can dribble or shoot with both feet or only one. If the player is much stronger with one foot, then you should focus on that side. Try to pick up that information early on by watching the player.

Like goalies, fullbacks often have the chance to launch a counterattack. As a general rule, as soon as you get the ball you should try to clear it toward the sidelines and down the field to a teammate who is open. Sometimes, when you're playing deep near your own goal and the other team is applying pressure, you may not have the time to pick out a target or even to get control of the ball. In that situation, you'll simply want to kick the ball as hard as you can, doing your best to angle your shot toward the sidelines and down the field.

A fullback should be able to figure out in advance where the action is going to be and go aggressively after every loose ball in the area. A fullback should also be able to challenge forwards around the goal area by using a technique called heading. This means intercepting a shot with your head and directing it down the field. Here's a brief summary of your job as a fullback:

- Stop the other team from taking a shot on goal.
- Stay between your opponent and the goal.
- Try to stop the pass.
- Guide the dribbler toward the sidelines.
- Provide support for your teammates.
- Clear the ball from your defensive area with smart passes.

Midfielders

Midfielders are also called *halfbacks* because they are half fullback and half forward. Midfielders roam up and down and across the field, playing a defensive role when the other team has the ball and organizing the attack when their team gets the ball. Ideally, a midfielder combines the best qualities of Lawrence Taylor of pro football's New York Giants and Magic Johnson of pro basketball's Los Angeles Lakers—ferocious and stalking on defense, creative at passing, dribbling and scoring on offense.

Many soccer experts will tell you that the team that controls the midfield area will usually win the game. That makes perfect sense. It means that the ball is being kept out of a team's defensive area and in its opponent's end. The more often a ball is in the attacking zone, the more

Midfielders—the vital link between forwards and fullbacks, and between offense and defense.

often you will have the chance to score.

Generally speaking, as a midfielder you should always keep the ball in front of you. This means that your first responsibility is to think defensively. You don't want to get trapped upfield (toward your opponent's goal) and find yourself unable to help the fullbacks if the other team gets the ball.

When the ball is safely in front of you, you should use all your offensive skills to help make scoring opportunities. Most of the time those opportunities will be used by a forward, but a skilled halfback will also wind up with plenty of shots on goal.

Forwards

Forwards must be terrific scorers. Different coaches and systems call forwards by different names and assign different responsibilities. But above all else forwards must be able to put the ball in the net.

Most teams use between three and five forwards at a time. The outside forwards are usually called *wingers*. The inside forwards are often called *center forwards* or *strikers*.

The chief areas of responsibility for wingers are the areas near the sidelines. Wingers should be good dribblers and shooters so they can beat their defenders and slice in for shots on goal. They should also be very good at making crossing passes so they can get the ball to center forwards near the goal. Wingers must be good runners and have a lot of stamina.

A team's best scorers usually play in the center forward

position. Because center forwards must have the ball in order to score, they have to be good at ball collecting, also known as gaining control of the ball, which will be explained in the next chapter. They also must develop the ability to move *without* the ball and position themselves where they are in shooting range of the goal and in passing range of the ball.

If you play striker, you should be quick and have good reflexes. During games, the opportunity to shoot often lasts for only a second. As a forward you should practice kicking for speed as well as accuracy. Set up a bunch of balls in a semi-circle inside the penalty area. As quickly as you can, run to each ball and take a shot on goal. Keep a record of how many goals you score and how quickly you go around the circle. But don't sacrifice accuracy for speed. And, remember to practice kicking balls in the air and on the bounce.

Forwards should also know when *not* to shoot. If you are out of your shooting range, don't waste a scoring opportunity for your team by taking a weak shot. Pass the ball to a teammate who is in a better position.

When shooting don't kick the ball right at the goalie. Always kick to a spot in the back of the net. And always follow your shots in, looking for a rebound.

As forward, you also have some defensive responsibilities. As soon as the other team gets the ball, you have to become a defender. If the ball is near you, challenge the player who has it. If the ball is not in your immediate area, move toward it and block a possible passing lane. Don't mope around or lose your cool after a bad shot or a poor pass. Go get the ball back and do your stuff!

Forwards are a soccer team's goal machines, the wingers and strikers who streak downfield trying to score.

Chapter 6

SKILLS AND DRILLS

Many important soccer skills have been mentioned as we've discussed the players and their responsibilities. In this chapter the skills are broken down so you can work toward mastering them. They are all necessary if you want to become a complete soccer player, but you don't have to learn them all at once. You should work at your own pace and in a way that makes you feel comfortable.

Passing

The game of soccer is based on the skill of passing. It is the fastest way to move a ball out of danger and into scoring position, but it requires teamwork.

Although you can and should use your head to pass, we will discuss that later in this chapter. Right now we will concentrate on using your feet.

A pass has two parts. They are the *strike*, kicking the ball to a teammate, and the *reception*, when the teammate receives the ball. You don't just kick the ball; it has to be directed at its target. A pass must be accurate, kicked *to* a place with the proper speed so that your teammate can receive it easily. When you pass to a teammate who is on the move, he should not have to slow down to receive it. It is also important to remember that what you do with your *non*-kicking foot is just as important as what you do with your kicking foot. Here are some tips to keep in mind while you practice your passing:

● Always pick a specific spot on the ball that you are going to strike. Keep your eyes on that spot until you have kicked it.

● Always place your non-kicking foot 4 to 8 inches from the ball and point it in the direction that you want the kick to go.

● Hold your ankle stiff when you kick the ball. If it isn't locked and rigid when you strike, the kick will be weak and the ball won't hit its target.

● When you kick the ball, make sure that you are leaning slightly forward. If you don't lean into the kick, you'll lose power and you won't be able to follow through.

You can use different parts of the foot to kick a pass, every part *but* the toe. The following section explains how best to use the different parts of your foot.

The Inside-of-the-foot Pass

This is the most common type of pass, and the most accurate. Because you can't generate much power with it, it is only used to make relatively short passes. But despite the lack of power, the *inside-of-the-foot pass* is *the* basic method of moving the ball around and developing a team's attack on goal. Here's how it works:

1. Place your non-kicking foot on the side of the ball, about 4 to 6 inches away from it. With your knee slightly bent, point that foot in the direction you want the ball to travel.

2. Now turn your kicking foot *so that the inside of the foot is lined up with the back of the ball.*

3. Keep your ankle stiff so that you get power and can control the direction of the ball.

4. Keep your eye on the center of the ball.

5. Move your kicking foot back and off the ground.

The inside-of-the-foot pass

6. *Kick through the center of the ball; this means, don't change your leg's movement when your foot makes contact. Keep your leg moving as though the ball wasn't there, and don't finish the kick until your leg won't go any higher. That's called following through.*

The Instep Pass

Most people have a natural inclination to kick a soccer ball with their toes, but that is wrong. You can't *control* the ball if you are kicking with your toes, because so little of your foot comes into contact with the ball. The correct way to boot a hard pass is to use your instep—the top part of your foot in front of your ankle. You also use the instep when you want to generate a powerful kick.

1. Place your non-kicking foot alongside the ball, and

point your toes in the direction you want the pass to go.

2. Bring your kicking foot back by bending your knee. Your foot should be pointed straight down.

3. Keep your eye on the center of the ball.

4. Swing the foot forward, keeping your ankle locked. You should strike the ball in the center, with the top of your instep.

5. Follow through.

A lot of players find it helpful to hold their arms out from their sides to maintain their balance. It also may help to approach the kick from a slight angle. If you do it that

The instep pass

65

way, lean slightly away from the ball and turn your kicking foot slightly outward. Then follow the steps listed above.

One way to get comfortable with this technique is to practice it while someone holds the ball. The person can sit down and hold the ball in place while you concentrate on the kick. Take one step toward the ball and then kick. Keep repeating this drill until you get comfortable with it.

The Outside-of-the-foot Pass

This pass is useful when you're dribbling up the field and want to make a quick pass to a teammate running up the sideline. It's also important because it is the basic pass to use off the high-speed dribble, which we'll discuss later.

The outside-of-the-foot pass

1. Place your non-kicking foot to the side and a little behind the ball. The inside of your non-kicking foot (not the toes this time) should face where you want the pass to go.

2. Lifting your foot off the ground, point the toes of your kicking foot down and turn your ankle in.

3. Keeping your eye on the center of the ball and your ankle locked, bend your knees and raise your foot so that it is even with the center of the ball.

4. Kick through the center of the ball using the outside of your foot (from right behind the little toe).

5. Follow through. At first, passing with the outside of the foot is going to feel awkward, and you may not be able to generate a lot of power. Be patient. Keep practicing (and keep that ankle locked) and you'll get there.

Passing Drills

Tape a target to the bottom of a wall and practice kicking the ball at the target from about 10 feet away. (Make sure that it's O.K. to use the wall before you start bouncing soccer balls off it!) Start with the inside-of-the-foot kick, then try the outside-of-the-foot and the instep kicks. Remember to concentrate on proper kicking techniques, including keeping your eye on the ball until you strike it. Practice the kicks with one foot, then the other. It will seem awkward at first to use the foot that you don't normally use. But if you are able to perform soccer skills with *either* foot, you'll be that much more of a threat on the field in a game. So keep working at it, and you'll see quite a difference in a few weeks, and so will your teammates and opponents!

When you can regularly hit the target 8 out of 10 times, increase the distance to 20 feet. If you don't have a convenient wall, you can put a stick in the ground and use that as your target. What's important is *how* you're kicking, not what you're kicking at.

Here are some details to keep in mind:

- Are you keeping your ankle locked?
- Are you following through?
- When you practice the inside-of-the-foot pass, are the toes of your non-kicking foot pointed toward the target?
- When you practice the outside-of-the-foot pass, is the arch of your non-kicking foot pointing toward the target?

If you have a friend to practice with, the two of you can stand about 10 feet apart and pass to each other with each of you stopping the ball as you receive the pass. Practice the three basic kicks 10 to 15 times each, using both feet to pass and stop the ball. Concentrate on your technique, including the speed of your passes. You want the ball to have as much pace as your partner can handle.

When you have reached the point where you can easily pass, increase the distance from 10 to 20 feet. But don't be in a rush to increase the distance. Good form and accuracy are what count.

After you feel very comfortable with your passing, you can vary your practice sessions by trying what is called a *one-touch* drill. Instead of stopping the ball when you receive a pass, pass the ball back while it's still rolling. Start at 10 feet and use each of the three basic passing techniques. This drill is an excellent way to simulate game conditions.

If your passes are going off to one side, it means that

? *WHAT IF* I get hurt?

You can avoid some injuries by keeping in good shape and warming up before every game and practice. But if you play enough ball, you my get injured.

If you get hurt during a game, don't try to play through the pain. Stop playing and let the referee know that you're injured. If you go down during a game or practice and feel pain or dizziness, *don't* try to get up. Stay where you are and wait for your coach or the referee to check you out. And if you need medical attention, be sure to follow the doctor's instructions and give yourself enough time to heal completely.

you're either not pointing the toes of your non-kicking foot correctly, forgetting to lock the ankle of your kicking foot, or not striking the ball with the correct part of the foot.

If your passes are bouncing along the ground rather than rolling, then you're kicking the ball above its center. And if your passes are going up in the air, then you're striking it below the center. Remember, the ball only goes where you send it. It's a good idea for you and your partner to agree to point out each other's mistakes in a *constructive* way. Never make fun of someone's efforts, and never allow someone to make fun of yours. You're not in competition with anyone else. You're just trying to learn to be the best soccer player that *you* can be. You'll get there at your own pace.

Dribbling

In soccer, dribbling is the technique of moving the ball with a series of little kicks. Learning to dribble well is one of the keys to becoming a complete soccer player. Knowing *when* to dribble is also very important.

In most situations when you have the ball, you should be looking either to pass to a teammate who is open or to take a shot on goal if you are in good position. But there are situations in which dribbling is better than passing or shooting. These situations are:

- When you can't pass to your teammates because they

When defenders swarm around you, the inside-of-the-foot dribble is your best bet for controlling the ball and getting out of trouble. Try to make a pass in this situation.

are all being marked by opponents.

- When you want to avoid being tackled.

- When you have some space and your team has just started to organize its attack.

- When you see an opportunity to draw a defender away from a teammate who will then be in a good position to receive a pass.

- When you are on a breakaway (meaning you've "broken away" from the pack and are running alone or with just one other player) with perhaps only a fullback and a goalie to beat.

In a way, dribbling, although an essential skill, is a last resort, something you do to give yourself the space to make a pass or take a shot. Too much dribbling slows a team down. And the longer you dribble, the more likely it is that you will be challenged for the ball by the other team and end up turning it over to your opponents.

An important element in dribbling is to build up a rhythm or get in a groove. That means not just kicking the ball at random but keeping it under such tight control that it almost feels like a yo-yo tied to your feet by an invisible string.

Try not to watch the ball while you're dribbling. You might not feel comfortable with this at first, but it should be your long-term goal. Remember, dribbling is simply a way to get yourself into position to make a pass or take a shot. If you are watching the ball, you can't see an open teammate or the goal or opponents moving in to take the ball away.

Keep in mind that if you kick the ball too hard when you're dribbling, you will probably lose control of it and have it taken away. Likewise, if you kick the ball too softly, you won't be able to move very fast and you will quickly be challenged. Try to keep the ball about a foot or two in front of you.

Don't worry about speed when you first begin to practice. Start out at a walking pace and work up to a jog.

The outside-of-the-foot dribble is the perfect technique to use when you are in open space or when you want to move quickly

Concentrate on dribbling correctly, at a pace that's comfortable for you. If you learn how to do it right, and keep practicing, the speed will come. At first you will need to keep your eye on the spot that you're going to strike—the center of the ball about an inch off the ground.

The first dribble to practice is the *inside-of-the-foot*

past an opponent. Notice that the eyes of this player are focused upfield, not on the ball.

dribble. To do this, you need to use *both* of your feet. You move the ball ahead by tapping it first with the inside of one foot (where the arch of your foot is) and then with the inside of your other foot. You should tap the ball forward just hard enough so you can reach it with one step before tapping it with your other foot. You should strike the ball only about an inch off the ground. Don't forget to lock your ankle. And don't try to keep the ball going in an absolutely straight line, or you'll look like a duck waddling back and forth. The ball should be kicked in a zig-zag pattern. When you feel comfortable dribbling at a jogging pace, kick a little harder so that you can run two strides before tapping the ball again.

The inside-of-the-foot dribble is used when speed is *not* important. It is used to maneuver in traffic and to go around an opponent, and is especially useful in combination with feints (which is what you do to "fake out" your opponent and which will be discussed later).

When speed *is* important, and you have the opportunity to run in the open field, you should use the *outside-of-the-foot dribble.* The technique for this is similar to how you move the ball in kicking or passing situations, but you *don't* follow through. If you did, the ball would roll too far ahead. Just turn your toes in and tap the ball with the outside of your foot. Keep your ankle locked, and strike the ball in the center, one inch above the ground. Instead of alternating taps with each foot, practice the dribble with one foot, and then switch to the other. Start with walkthroughs. When that feels comfortable, try to dribble while jogging. Before you know it, you will be pushing the ball up the field at a good pace. When you're really going at full speed, you should be pushing the ball about three or four steps ahead of you.

While you're dribbling, you should keep your body between the ball and the defender. This technique is known as *shielding* the ball—your body is the shield. Because your opponents aren't going to try to tackle you from only one side, you can see why you need to be skillful with both feet.

Changing the speed and direction of the dribble is another way to keep control of the ball. When you are coming close to a defender, vary your speed. For example, approach the defender at a jog, and when you are very close, pick up your pace and dribble right past him. Changing the pace usually catches the defender off-guard and buys you a step or two. You should also try changing direction. Here's a technique you can use while dribbling with the outside of your foot:

Dribble for three or four touches, and as you approach the ball for your next touch, pivot on your *non*-kicking foot and continue your dribble so that you are facing in a different direction. (Use the ball of your foot as the pivot.) Then tap the ball with the outside of your kicking foot, guiding it in that new direction. If you want to make a sharp turn, pivot 90 degrees; if you want to make only a slight change, pivot 45 degrees. In either case, continue your dribble as soon as you pivot. This technique is very similar to a basketball move known as a crossover dribble. Practice changing speed and direction by yourself and then with a defender.

To become a really accomplished dribbler, you also have to know how to avoid and how to move past oppo-

Stopping short and then picking up the dribble in a new direction is a great way to catch a defender off-guard— but only if you can control the ball and make quick decisions about what to do next!

nents by *feinting* them out of position. The purpose of the feint, or *fake*, is to confuse your opponents into thinking you are going in a particular direction or speed and then doing something different before they can react. The fake is designed to "freeze" your opponents for just the second it takes for you to explode past them.

The head-and-shoulder fake is a basic fake that is used in basketball and football as well as in soccer. Practice it by dribbling close to someone who is acting as a defender. When you are a few steps away, drop one shoulder and lean your head to that same side. The defender will probably lean that way, too, which allows you to dribble around him on the other side.

Another basic fake you can use when you are speed dribbling and about to be overtaken by a defender is to stop the ball suddenly by placing your foot on top of the ball. The idea is for the defender to keep running a few steps after you've stopped, leaving you free to pass the ball or to pick up the dribble in another direction. A good variation, after you have shown a defender this move once, is to *fake* stepping on the ball, and when the defender slows down, pick up the dribble *without* stopping. A word of warning: When you first try stepping on the ball, make sure that you and the ball aren't going too fast, or you might end up on your back.

Dribbling Drills

Dribbling drills are an excellent way to help you develop the staying power and leg strength you'll need during games. In the beginning, just work on mastering the techniques. Concentrate on tapping the ball in the right place with the proper part of your foot. Work on keeping the ball under control. *Don't* be concerned with speed. Walk through each drill and *gradually* build up to jogging and then to full speed. Go at your own pace. Use both the inside-of-the-foot dribble and the outside-of-the-foot dribble for each drill. Don't forget to use both feet!

Dribble straight ahead for 15 to 20 yards, then turn and come back. Repeat 10 times with the inside of the foot and with the outside of the foot, 5 times with the left foot and 5 times with the right.

After you've been practicing your straight-ahead dribbling for a while, and you're able to move fairly quickly and keep the ball under control, set up an obstacle course by sticking some pieces of wood into the ground. (If you can get traffic cones, that would be even better.) Arrange them in a winding pattern that looks like one capital letter S on top of another, or like a snake lying out in the sun. Put a net or a target near the end of the last obstacle. Then dribble the ball around the obstacles. Each time you dribble through the course without losing control of the ball, reward yourself with a shot on goal.

Once you're comfortable dribbling the ball at a fast pace with both feet, you should practice against a defender. The defender should cover you loosely, and not try to take the ball away at first. This is known as *shadow training*. Whenever you practice a new skill against a defender, it should start out as a *shadow drill* so you can develop your technique. In the next phase, the defender should get closer to you but still not try to take the ball. This is known as *passive-resistance training*. In the third phase, the defender should react as if it was a game and work at taking the ball from you.

Collecting

Because soccer is based on the ability of a team to pass, players have to know how to "catch," or receive, a pass. In soccer the term for catching is *collecting*. Some people also use the word *trapping*.

Collecting means bringing a moving ball under control before putting it back into play. The idea is to stop the ball and then put it back into play—either with a pass, a dribble or a shot—in one smooth motion. In order to do this, the part of your body that receives the ball has to "give" as soon as the ball hits it. If you don't cushion the contact, the ball will bounce away as though it had struck a backboard.

In soccer, you use your feet, shins, thighs, chest and head to collect. We'll discuss collecting with your feet in this section and cover the other body parts in Chapter 7.

Collecting with the *inside* of the foot is the most useful trap to learn. Here's how to do it:

1. Face in the direction the ball is coming from.

2. Turn your collecting foot the way you would to make an inside-of-the-foot pass, and put it slightly in front of your other foot.

3. Bending your knee slightly, raise the collecting foot a few inches off the ground so that it is at the same height as the center of the ball. If you don't raise your foot at all, the ball will just roll over your shoe. If you raise it too

Collecting (or trapping) the ball with the inside of the foot, the most commonly used technique for receiving a pass

high, the ball may go right under your foot. That could be very embarrassing!

4. Line up the collecting foot so that the ball hits between the base of your big toe and your ankle.

5. Lock your ankle, and just as the ball strikes, pull your foot back. That backward action will cushion the force and keep the ball from ricocheting off your foot. This will allow you to control the ball.

6. As soon as you have control of the ball, be prepared to take action: pass, dribble or shoot.

You can use the same basic technique to collect a ball that is in the air, but you will have to bend your knee a lot more. The speed of the ball determines how sharply you have to pull your foot back. The faster the ball is moving toward you, the faster you'll have to pull your foot back to have it act as a cushion.

To collect a ground ball with the *outside* of the foot, use the top of your foot between the base of your little toe and your ankle. Turn your non-collecting foot slightly to the outside, with the knee bent a bit. Raise your trapping foot a few inches off the ground, swivel your hips away from the ball, point your toes down and to the inside and lock your ankle. As the ball strikes, pull your foot back.

When you start practicing, concentrate on learning the proper technique. Keep in mind that when you collect in a game you need to check what's going on around you *before* the ball actually arrives so that you'll know what to do with it after you collect it. The sequence should be:

1. *Scan the field before you receive the ball.*
2. *Collect the ball.*
3. *Make your move instantly.*

This all takes time to put together in one package, so just take a deep breath and relax. Be patient with yourself, and don't give up.

Collecting Drills

To perform these drills, you're going to need another person to practice with. If you don't have a soccer-playing friend around, maybe someone in your family can help.

For the first drill, have the other person stand 15 feet away from you and roll the ball to you (this is called serving). Practice collecting with both the inside and outside parts of each foot. Remember to keep your collecting ankle locked and to cushion the impact by pulling your foot back as soon as the ball touches it. After you collect the ball, return it to the server using the passes you've been practicing.

The person doing the serving should start off rolling the ball slowly, and then move on to faster and more varied serves. When you feel comfortable with your technique and can consistently control the ball, have the server start to throw the ball a few feet away from you so that you can practice collecting on the move.

Shooting

It's important to master all soccer skills. But scoring goals is still the ultimate aim of a soccer team, and that can only be done with good strong shooting.

Most goals are scored from within the penalty box, and it's usually pretty crowded in there. If you want to become a successful goal scorer you will have to develop a *quick*, *hard* and *accurate* kick.

When you take a shot you shouldn't just kick in the general direction of the goal. And you shouldn't kick right at the goalkeeper. That might sound obvious, but a surprising number of players shoot as if the ball was a magnet and the goalie was made of iron.

Don't make life easy for the goalie. Pick a target area at the back of the net and kick for that target. This will help your accuracy and force you to lean into the kick and follow through. A powerful kick gives the goalie less time to react.

Remember, don't stare at the net. As you go to kick, keep your eye on the center of the ball, not the goal. Your *immediate* target is the ball. If you keep your head down, your eye on the center of the ball and your feet in the proper position, the ball will find its mark.

Use the instep shot, like the instep pass, when you want distance and power. Remember to keep your eye on the center of the ball, to keep your ankle locked and to follow through.

The same basic kicks that are used for passing are also used for shooting, and the mechanics are the same. Most shots on goal come from instep kicks because it is the most powerful method of kicking. Remember to bend slightly at the waist, bring your leg back with the knee down sharply and strike *through* the center of the ball.

The inside-of-the-foot shot is taken when you are very close to the goal and accuracy is more important than power. The time to use this kick for a shot on goal is, for example, when you are alone with the ball on one side of the net while the goalkeeper is trapped out of position on the other side or down on the ground. In that case, you should be willing to sacrifice some power to gain accuracy.

The inside-of-the-foot shot is also good to use off the dribble when you are coming in one-on-one against the goalie, because you can get the shot off fast. Lots of times you can catch the goalie moving out at you to block the shot. When the goalie does this, you can simply direct your shot around him.

Don't try to force shots just because you want to get slaps on the back from your teammates. Forced shots don't usually go in; they get blocked or saved. That means you've turned the ball over to your opponents, which won't make you too popular with your teammates or coach. Everyone likes to score, but in a team game, it doesn't matter which player scores. You win or lose as a team. So if you aren't in a good position, or if you see that a teammate has a better scoring opportunity, *pass* the ball. Besides, passing is contagious. The more you pass, the more likely it is that teammates will pass to you.

Shooting Drills

Although it's important to practice shooting with all three parts of your feet (the inside, outside and instep), you should spend most of your practice time on the instep shot because that's the one you will use most often in games. If you have trouble with the instep kick at first, ask someone to hold the ball for you while you practice kicking it correctly.

If you are practicing by yourself, you can tape two targets to a wall. The targets should be about 3 feet off the ground and about 5 feet apart. Pretend one of the targets is the goalie and the other is a spot at the back of the net. Stand 10 feet away and alternate kicking at each of the targets so that you'll get used to shooting at different parts of the "net." Place the ball at different spots on the ground, and shoot from different angles. As you get the hang of it, move back until you are the same distance from the target as the penalty spot is from the goal in your league. But work your way back gradually, and never increase the distance until you have achieved consistent technique and accuracy.

Remember to practice with both feet. Although using your weaker foot will probably be very frustrating for a while, soon it will feel natural and you will become a much better player.

If you don't have a wall, make a target area using a large piece of wood, or even two sticks in the ground. Maybe you can save up for a small practice net. It doesn't really matter what you use; the idea is to use it.

When you practice with a friend, you can take turns

being the shooter and the goalie. The goalie should roll the ball out and the other player should first collect and then shoot. You can reward yourselves with a shot when you have collected properly.

Heading

Heading is a technique used for passing or taking a shot on goal, using only your head. The four most important points to remember about heading are as follows:

1. You should not let the ball hit you; you must strike the ball.

2. You must keep your eyes open.

3. You have to keep your hands and arms away from the ball.

4. The only part of your head that you use in heading is the forehead, the area between your eyebrows and your hairline.

Some coaches have new players grab the front of their jerseys when they're going to head the ball. This prevents players from using their arms as a shield at the last second.

The proper stance for heading involves arching your back slightly backward, bending your knees, rising on the balls of your feet and holding your neck stiff. When the ball comes at you, keep your eyes on it and then move your head forward sharply. Don't forget to keep your neck stiff; if you bend your neck, the ball will hit the top of your head.

If you head the ball properly, it *will not* hurt you. A lot of beginning players don't believe this. If you're worried about being injured, let some air out of your ball to make

The proper technique for heading the ball

it softer before you practice, or try a beach ball. Some beginning players put a small piece of tape on their foreheads, making it easier to practice striking the ball with the proper area of the head.

In the beginning, you should only be concerned with developing the proper striking technique. As soon as you get that, you should begin to use the header to pass the ball, or if you are within range, to take a shot. Of course, this means that you will have to scan the field before you head the ball so you know where the players around you are positioned. Do *not* attempt to head balls that are below your chest—you could be kicked in the head by accident.

Heading Drills

When you're alone you can practice heading by tossing the ball into the air. (If you happen to have a tetherball set, you can also use that for practicing your heading. You won't have to keep chasing the ball.) Keep your eyes open, your knees bent, your back arched, you head back and your neck rigid. Don't forget to use your forehead and to hit *up* at the ball; don't let it just bounce off you.

As soon as you feel comfortable, set up a target and try heading the ball at the target. Remember, the purpose of heading is to complete a pass or take a shot on goal. Always keep your eyes on the ball.

When you're practicing with someone else you can take turns serving to each other. In one drill, the server doubles as the goalie which allows the player doing the heading to

---

? WHY DON'T I seem to be improving?

Don't be impatient. Becoming good at any sport takes time. If you really want to play and enjoy the game, just keep trying to be the best player you can be. Some players improve more slowly than others, just as some people grow more slowly. Keep at it and don't get discouraged.

Not too long ago there was a boy in the pee-wee leagues who was so uncoordinated that he had trouble just trying to kick the ball. He also was so weak that when he *did* manage to get his foot on the ball, it only moved a few feet. But he always came to practice and always tried his best. The next year was much like the first, but he kept working on his skills. By the following year his body strength and coordination increased and all his practicing paid off. He was playing center forward and taking his team's penalty shots.

*Heading in a game is a lot different than in practice.
There'll probably be another head up there with you!*

try to score. In another drill the server moves after the toss and the other player tries to head-pass the ball to where the server has moved. When you feel comfortable heading from a stationary position, the server should toss the ball so that you have to take a step or two to reach it.

Juggling

Juggling is the technique of keeping the ball in the air by using your feet, thighs and head in any combination. While juggling is not used very often in games, it is probably the best way for you to develop a feel for the ball and to gain an overall feeling of mastery in the other phases of the game.

To perfect the technique, you have to keep the areas of contact—the foot, the thigh, the head—horizontal, so that

Juggling with the thigh, one of the best ways to practice ball control

the ball goes straight up and down. If you tap the ball with a foot, thigh or head that's at an angle, the ball will bounce away. Don't forget to keep your eye on the ball.

To juggle with the instep, lift your foot a few inches off the ground and keep the foot level. As the ball comes down, strike it lightly, with your knee slightly bent.

To juggle with your thigh, bend your knee and lift your foot so that your thigh is level. As the ball comes down, strike it gently with the center of your thigh.

To juggle the ball with your head, bend your knees and arch your back slightly. As the ball comes down, tilt your head back, raise the heels of your feet and tap the ball with your forehead.

Juggling Drills

To practice juggling, drop the ball onto your instep and gently tap it back up. Keep the taps low, and don't forget to keep your toes pointed straight out and your eye on the ball. Spend a few minutes on the instep, and then move on to the thigh and the head.

Juggling isn't easy at first, but as you keep practicing you will be amazed at how long you can keep the ball in the air! After you've practiced a few days, set yourself a goal of five consecutive taps. Then try to increase it by one tap every day.

When you feel comfortable juggling in place, try it while walking. You should also practice combination juggling: alternate tapping the ball between your head, thighs and insteps. Remember that in a game, the idea is to get the ball to where you can do something with it, and juggling can help you set up a shot or a pass.

Juggling with the instep, and with the thigh, head and chest, should be part of your practice routine. See how many taps you can make before the ball hits the ground!

Tackling

In soccer, tackling is the technique used for taking the ball away from an opponent (without using your hands or arms, of course). The idea is to catch your opponent off-balance while he is dribbling the ball. There are four basic tackles:

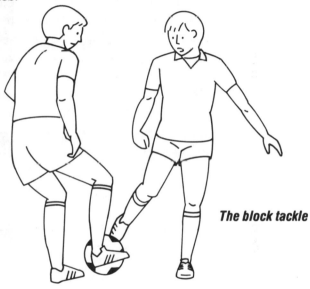

The block tackle

1. The Block Tackle: After watching your opponent dribble the ball, you figure out when he is going to kick the ball next and challenge him for the ball by kicking it with the inside of your foot at the same time.

2. The Poke Tackle: This is the same idea as the block tackle, except you poke the ball away from your opponent with your toes instead of the inside of your foot.

3. The Slide Tackle: In this move, you actually slide

toward your opponent and kick the ball away. The slide is similar to the feet-first one used in baseball. Practice the sliding technique without a defender before you try to use it in a game. You slide on your side, feet first. Bend your top leg at the knee and then, with that leg, kick through the ball with your instep. You should also use your inside arm to cushion your slide along the ground and help you maintain balance. If you have never been taught to slide properly, check with your coach before you practice this technique. It's important to remember these two facts about the slide tackle:

● If you miss the tackle, your opponent is on the loose and is not being covered by you. You should never use this technique when you're the last defender, unless it's the only chance you have to prevent the breakaway.

● If you miss the ball but hit your opponent, you may be penalized for kicking or tripping. And be extra careful

The slide tackle

about using a slide tackle in your own penalty area, where fouls result in penalty kicks.

4. The Shoulder Charge: This is the only way you can legally make body contact with an opponent on a soccer field. In the shoulder charge, you bump your shoulder into an opponent's shoulder. The idea is to knock your opponent off balance and gain control of the ball for yourself or a teammate. The shoulder charge may be used when you are running alongside an opponent. You should lift your outside foot (the foot that's farthest away from your opponent), bend your inside knee and lean into your opponent. Keep these important points in mind:

● Always keep your arms down at your sides. If you strike with your elbow, you can be called for a foul.

● You may not take a long run at your opponent before using a shoulder charge. You have to be within what is called *playing distance*, about three or four feet.

● Remember: The idea behind a shoulder charge is to get the ball away, not to play bumper cars. Don't get into a bumping contest. Knock your opponent off balance and then quickly go after the ball.

One last word about tackling: The techniques discussed here are essential skills to learn. But tackling is risky and should be done more or less as a last resort. First try to force your opponent to go where he doesn't want to go by positioning your body correctly. The basic idea of defensive soccer is to control where the attacker can and cannot go. It's only when you can't contain an opponent any other way that you move in for a tackle.

Chapter 7

ADVANCED SKILLS AND DRILLS

Before you practice these advanced skills, you should already be able to do the basic skills discussed in the last chapter. If you practice these drills with a friend, you can take turns acting as server and kicker, as you did before. The server can also double as a goalie.

The Chip

The purpose of this kick is to lift the ball up over an opponent's head and have it come quickly down again. Forwards like to use it for shots on goal when the goalie strays too far out of the goal area. It is important, though, that the ball go up and *down*; otherwise you'll kick the ball over the net. The kick is done as follows:

1. Stand with your non-kicking foot next to the ball.

2. Bring the knee of your kicking leg as far back as you can.

The chip shot; note the lack of a follow-through

3. Swing your foot and leg down with a quick jabbing motion. Don't follow through. The idea is to get your foot under the ball and to lift it by hitting it with the flat part of your foot right behind your toes.

When you practice the chip, make sure you slide your toes under the ball. When you can get the ball in the air and in the direction that you want it to go 7 out of 10 times, have someone serve to you and practice chipping a moving ball.

The Volley

You volley the ball when you kick it while it is still in the air. Depending upon the flight of the ball, your position and what you want to do with your kick, you can use either your instep or the inside of your foot. When you volley the ball you use the same technique as when the ball is on the ground, but you kick the ball when it is at about shin-height.

1. Point your non-kicking foot toward the ball.

2. As the ball comes down keep your head down and your eye on the ball.

3. If you're kicking with the inside of your foot, turn your kicking foot sideways and lock that ankle the way you would on a ground ball. If you're using your instep, keep the foot straight and ankle locked.

4. For added power pick up the heel of your non-kicking foot a moment before you strike the ball.

5. As the ball drops down, kick right through the center with a big follow-through.

The volley kick

You can practice the volley by dropping a ball and kicking it at a goal or target before it hits the ground. Start at about 10 feet away. After you get the hang of it and are kicking the ball accurately, start moving back 5 feet at a time.

The Half Volley

Use your instep to make this kick *right after the ball has bounced,* when it is about an inch or two off the ground.

1. Judge where the ball is about to bounce and start your kick before the ball touches the ground.

2. Make sure that your toes are pointed down and that you have a short follow-through. This way you will con-

trol the ball and keep it from flying over your teammates when you're passing or over the goal when you're shooting.

You can practice the half volley the same way you practice the volley, except that you let the ball hit the ground before you kick it.

The Wall Pass

In this play, a player makes a pass to a teammate, and then runs toward open space. The receiver quickly redirects the ball with a one-touch pass back to the first player, who is sprinting by. (In basketball this play is known as the give-and-go.)

To practice the wall pass you will need another player. Set up three sticks in a right triangle. Each of you stands in front of a stick, leaving one stick unattended. The receiving player makes a one-touch pass that should arrive at the open stick at the same time as the passing player. If you are practicing in a group of three, use four sticks and set up a square.

The Through Pass

This play is also known as the "killer pass," because of how deadly it can be to the defense. The play at its most effective sends a player in on goal on a breakaway.

Typically, a player *without* the ball makes a run toward the goal. Just before the player is about to run past the last fullback and be in an offside position, a teammate passes the ball through or over the defender or defenders. This play can also be used effectively in other areas of the field to break free from or confuse defenders. The through pass can effectively build up your attack.

The through pass requires at least three players to practice. You need a passer, someone to make the run and a defender. Timing is very important in this situation. As the two attackers approach the defender, they have to time the run and the pass so that the runner doesn't pass the defender before the ball does.

Collecting

Collecting airborne balls is more difficult than collecting ground balls. The part of the body you use depends on how the ball is coming toward you. For instance you will use your instep for low balls, your thigh or chest for mid-level balls, and your head for high balls.

Using the Instep

1. Hold your foot up and forward, as you would for a volley shot.

2. Point your toes toward the ground.

3. As soon as you touch the ball, pull your foot down. The ball will stick to your foot as though glued-on.

Using the Thigh

1. Stand with your feet shoulder-width apart.

2. As the ball comes down, lift one leg, bend the knee and point the toes downward, as you would if you were going to juggle.

3. As the ball hits the thigh, pull your leg down. The ball will drop at your feet.

This player makes a hard job look easy! But collecting the ball with the instep is only the first part of the play; now he has to get past the man marking him on defense.

When you raise your leg at the beginning of this technique, try to keep it loose. If you tense your muscles, you'll be giving the ball a wall rather than a pillow to land on and it will bounce away.

Using the Chest
To collect a high ball:

    1. Stand with your feet shoulder-width apart.

    2. Arch your body backward from the waist and bend your knees.

    3. As the ball is about to touch, take a deep breath.

    4. As soon as you feel the ball, let out your breath and straighten up. The ball should be right at your feet.

Remember to keep your arms spread out so that you don't get penalized for touching the ball with your hands.

**Collecting
with the chest;
left, for high balls;
right, for
bouncing balls**

To collect a ball that is bouncing up toward you:

1. Stand with your legs shoulder-width apart.

2. Bend slightly forward from the waist and take a deep breath.

3. Allow the ball to hit you in the chest. Remember to keep your arms away from your body.

Using the Head

Use your head to collect when you're not in a position to shoot and there isn't a teammate around to pass to.

1. Position your head so that the ball will strike the top of your forehead.

2. At the moment of contact, pull your head slightly back to cushion the impact.

To practice collecting airborne balls, you'll need someone to serve them to you. The balls should be thrown at various heights and from different distances and angles, so that you get to practice under every circumstance. Use your feet, thighs, chest and head. After you have mastered collecting while you're standing still, the server should begin throwing balls that force you to collect on the move.

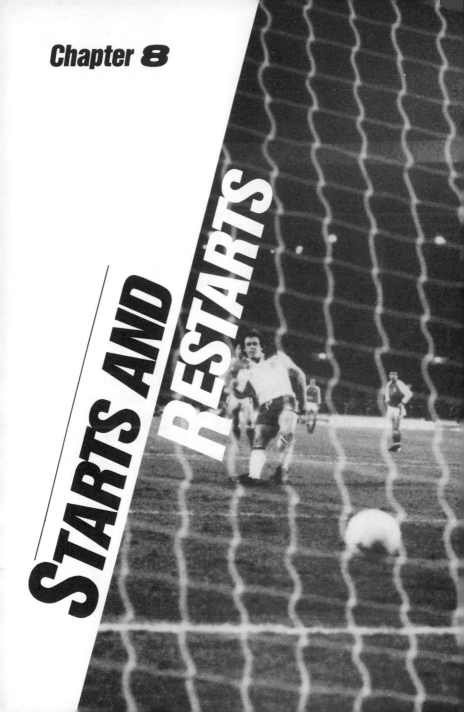

Chapter 8

STARTS AND RESTARTS

In this chapter we discuss a group of plays called starts and restarts, which occur when the ball is put into motion and play begins. These special situations are vital for a team to master because *more than 50 percent* of all goals scored are a direct result of starts and restarts.

The Kickoff

The kickoff is the play that starts the game. It also starts the second half, and is used after every goal. Unlike American football, in soccer the team kicking off tries to keep possession of the ball, and doesn't automatically boot it away to the other team.

At the beginning of the game the referee calls the captains to the middle of the field for a coin toss. The team that wins the toss chooses whether to kick off or defend the goal of his choice. In the second half the teams switch sides, and the team that didn't take the opening kickoff takes it to start the second half.

For the kickoff the referee places the ball on the center spot. Each team must have all its players in its own half of the field. All the players on the team *not* taking the kickoff must be at least 10 yards away from the ball until it is put into play.

After the referee blows the whistle the kicking team puts the ball into play with a kick. The ball must travel *forward* at least the distance of its own circumference (about two feet), and the kicker may not touch the ball until it has been touched by another player. As soon as the ball goes at least the designated distance, the opposing team can charge in and try to take the ball away.

A typical kickoff play has the center forward nudging the ball ahead to another forward, who kicks the ball backward to the center halfback. The pass back gives the forwards time to make runs into their opponent's side of the field while the halfbacks organize the attack.

Once the game begins it continues non-stop unless:

- A goal is scored.
- The referee rules the ball out of bounds.
- The referee signals a penalty or foul.
- The referee stops play temporarily because of an injury.

After a goal is scored, the team that was scored upon takes the kickoff.

Out-of-bounds Plays

When the referee rules that the ball has completely crossed one of the sidelines, the team that did *not* touch it last gets to throw the ball in at the spot at which it crossed the line. There are very specific rules for how throw-ins must be done. If they are not done properly, the other team gets the ball. Here are the rules:

1. The thrower must face the field at the spot where the ball went out.

2. The ball must be held with both hands.

3. The player must throw the ball over his head.

4. Part of each foot must be on the ground, and both feet are to be placed on or behind the sideline.

5. The player who throws the ball in may not touch the ball again until another player—from either team—has touched it.

If your team is well coached and reacts quickly, the throw-in can lead to some exciting opportunities. The idea is to get the throw-in done as quickly as possible so that your team is on the attack before your opponents are in their proper defensive positions. To properly perform the throw-in:

The throw-in

1. *Place your hands behind and slightly to the sides of the ball. Your hands should form the letter "W" and your thumbs should almost be touching.*

2. *Keeping your legs together, bring the ball behind your head, arch your body backward, bend your knees and stand on your toes.*

3. *Snap your body up and bring the ball forward, using equal force with both arms.*

It's important to use the proper technique in order to get power and distance in your throws. Some players like

The running throw-in

to take a running throw-in. That's fine, but remember that you can't go over the sideline or beyond the spot where the ball went out. And you can't lift either foot completely off the ground when you throw the ball. If you do, you'll be called for a violation.

When the ball goes over one of the endlines, but not into the goal, the team that did *not* knock it out gains possession. If the attacking team touched the ball last, then the defending team is awarded a goal kick. If the ball last touched the defending team, then the attacking team is awarded a corner kick.

The Goal Kick

The team taking a goal kick may place the ball anywhere inside the goal area as long as it's on the side on which the ball went out. The kick may be taken by any player, but

Though the players forming this wall have been careful not to block the goalie's vision, the kicker will do his best to angle

the assignment is usually given to the goalie or one of the fullbacks, who are most skilled at taking long, powerful kicks. All opposing players must remain outside the penalty area until the ball clears the box. If the ball does not clear the box, or if the kicker touches the ball a second time before it clears the box, the kick must be taken again.

*the ball around or over them toward the net. The four
defenders are not permitted to move until the ball is touched.*

Free Kicks

When the referee blows the whistle and signals a foul, the
team that was fouled is awarded a *free kick*. As we
described in Chapter 4, the referee will award either a
direct free kick or an *indirect* free kick, depending on the

type of violation. The difference between the two kicks is that a goal may be scored directly off a direct free kick. An indirect free kick must be touched by at least one other player before a goal can be scored.

In either case, the referee places the ball at the location of the foul. Opponents must stay 10 yards from the ball until it has been put into play by being kicked the distance of its circumference.

When the offensive team is awarded an indirect free kick from a spot that is within 10 yards of the goal line, the defenders must stand on the goal line. When a kick is taken from a team's own penalty area, the ball must travel outside the penalty box to be considered in play.

When a penalty is called on the defensive team at a spot close to its own goal, the players will form a "wall" to defend against the kick. A wall consists of a group of players standing shoulder to shoulder in front of the goal. Their role is to help the goalie by blocking part of the goal area, giving the kicker a slimmer section of goal to shoot at. The goalie normally instructs the players where to build a wall, so that he is not shielded and can see the ball coming if it gets by the wall. The kicker will often try to chip the ball over the wall or curve the kick around it. Kicking straight into the wall is, of course, counter-productive.

Sometimes the team taking the free kick will try to confuse the defending team. One common tactic on a direct kick is to have two players approach the ball at the same time, from different angles. One player might run right over the ball without touching it, leaving the ball for the second player. Or the first player might kick the ball, with the second player serving only as a decoy. In either case, the defense can't react very quickly because it can't tell until the last moment which of the two players will actually take the kick.

On an indirect kick, which must touch another player before a goal can be scored, the same tactic is often used. Two players approach the ball at the same time. The first player to touch the ball touches it only slightly—in effect, teeing it up for the second player, who then takes a strong kick or shot on goal.

The Corner Kick

Corner kicks are taken from the corner area on the side of the goal where the ball went out of bounds. The player assigned to take the corner should have a strong, accurate kick. Usually the kicker will try to place the ball right in front of the goal, where four or five teammates should be waiting to take a shot. Really talented kickers can make the ball curve right into the goal. All defensive players must be 10 yards away from the ball until it is kicked.

The Penalty Kick

When the defensive team commits a major foul in its own penalty area, the offensive team gets a penalty kick. The kick is taken from the penalty spot. All other players must be outside the penalty area and at least 10 yards away from the ball. The goalie must stand with both feet on the goal line, and may not move off the line until the ball is kicked. No other players from either team can charge into the penalty area until the ball has been put into play. If a defensive player violates this rule and the kick is missed, the kicking team gets to take another penalty kick. If the kicking team enters the penalty box too quickly and a goal is scored, the goal is disallowed, but the shooter gets to kick again.

? WHY ME? *(Or, how I lost the game for my team.)*

When you've just let in a goal on an easy shot, or kicked a penalty shot over the net as time runs out, it may seem like the end of the world, especially if you don't get much support from your teammates. But never forget that individuals don't win or lose soccer games; *teams* win and lose games. If a team loses by one goal, there were probably other scoring opportunities during the game that weren't cashed in.

Everyone who plays enough ball is bound to make a mistake sooner or later, but that doesn't make that person a failure. When Kirk Gibson hit his dramatic two-out, ninth-inning home run in Game One of the 1988 World Series, he hit it off Dennis Eckersley, the best relief pitcher in the game. Eckersley had just established a playoff record by saving all four wins against the Boston Red Sox in the American League Championship. That one pitch didn't turn Eckersley into a loser.

Nobody and no team wins or loses all the time. Do your best in every game, and learn to accept the fact that winning and losing are two sides of the same coin. Sometimes the coin just lands on the wrong side for your team.

Drop Balls

When the officials can't decide which team knocked the ball out of bounds, the referee will call a drop ball. The referee will also call a drop ball after an injury has stopped play. A drop ball is like a jump ball in basketball or a face-off in hockey. The referee designates the spot, and one player from each team comes to that spot. All other players must be at least 10 yards away until the ball is put in play. The referee drops the ball, and the moment that it hits the ground, the two players are free to kick it. Practicing half-volley kicks will pay off when you have to kick a drop ball.

Chapter 9

PUTTING IT ALL TOGETHER

*I*n the earlier chapters, we have broken the game of soccer down into parts. Now let's look at the way the individual player functions within the team.

Defensive Tactics

Players get asked to do different things depending on who their coach is and what system of play is used. On defense, for example, your coach may play either a *man-to-man* (sometimes called person-to-person) or a *zone* defense. With man-to-man defense, you are assigned to mark a specific player wherever that player goes on the field. In a zone defense, you cover a certain area of the field and mark *any* players who come into that area. Some coaches use a combination zone and man-to-man strategy. Regardless of the structure of the defense, the basic principles remain the same.

When your team loses the ball, the first thing that should happen is that the defensive player who is closest to the ball should apply pressure to the player with the ball. At the same time, the rest of your defensive team should get into position between the ball and your own goal. The idea is to slow your opponents' attack. If you can't slow them down, players from your team will get trapped behind the ball, and the other team will wind up with a fast break.

If you are marking the player with the ball, you should keep trying to slow the attack by using good positioning and guiding the player to the sidelines. While you are doing that, the three or four teammates closest to you should be supplying defensive support by playing slightly off the players they are marking. That way they will be in position to intercept a pass or pick up the pressure if the player with the ball should beat you.

The purpose of defensive tactics is to prevent your opponents from scoring. Once they've crossed midfield, the best way to do this is for your team to concentrate its defense in the danger zone, which is the area in the center of the field inside and just outside of the penalty box. While you are trying to contain the attack, you should always be looking for an opportunity to take the ball away and put your team back on the attack.

Offensive Tactics

The fundamental idea on offense is to move the ball as quickly as possible into your opponents' zone and score a goal. But that doesn't mean that you should proceed recklessly or without support. Sometimes going as quickly as possible means moving *slowly* while you attempt to build up an attack. First, you should try to maneuver the ball into open space. At the same time, try to get your opponents out of position. The best way to do that is for you and your teammates to stay in motion and keep the ball moving. Movement puts pressure on the defense. It causes the defense to become confused, and pulls defensive players out of position.

If you have the ball, you can advance it either by dribbling or passing, while your teammates are supporting you by staying on the move—also called "making runs"— looking to create space for themselves and passing lanes for you. Keep in mind, though, that a well-kicked ball will outrun any player, so always make the pass your first option.

When you have the ball, it is very important that at least two or three teammates are supporting you by making their runs in areas where you can reach them with a pass. One of those players should be slightly behind you to pick up the ball if you lose control over it or if you are tackled. This support is necessary to keep the attack moving forward and prevent the defense from ganging up on you. Once your team has maneuvered the ball into your opponents' danger zone, finish off the attack with a powerful shot on goal.

It's Game Time!

In soccer, the twenty-two players are constantly moving and adjusting their own positions in relation to the positions of the other players as well as to the ball, which is also in nearly constant motion. In the wink of an eye, you can go from defender to attacker, from chaser to being chased, and then back again.

We've tried to give you some useful information to help you make the right decisions when you are out there on the field. Of course the best way to learn the game is to *play* the game. But before you put on your cleats and grab a ball, here are a few final suggestions:

• Concentrate and be aware of what is going on in the game at all times. The ball may seem very far away, but it travels very quickly. Keep thinking ahead and figure out what you're going to do if the ball comes to you.

• Communicate with your teammates. A couple of

terms are especially useful. For example if you see that a teammate who is dribbling is about to be overtaken, yell "Man on!" If you are running to an open space in the middle of the field and a teammate has the ball on a sideline, yell "Cross!" so that he knows to send a pass in your direction. Your coach will fill you in on any other terms you should use on the field.

• Remember that a soccer team is like a chain and every player is an important link. Be a strong link and a good teammate!

GLOSSARY

Attacker: a player who is moving into position to score

Attacking zone: the half of the field you are in when you're trying to score a goal

Ball denial: positioning yourself on defense in order to keep the ball away from an opposing player

Caution: when a referee calls a player for misconduct and issues a yellow card to the player

Crossing pass: sending the ball from the sideline to the center of the field; also called "centering"

Corner kick: a kick taken from the corner of the field by the attacking team when the defending team last touched the ball before it went over the endline

Clearing: when the defensive team kicks, throws or heads the ball out of the goal or penalty areas

Collecting: the technique of catching a soccer ball and bringing it under control

Covering: when a defensive player backs up a teammate

Curving the ball: kicking the ball so it curves as it travels through the air

Cutting down the angle: when a goalie moves out toward a shooter to limit the amount of goal available to the shooter

Direct free kick: a kick awarded to a team because of a major foul committed by its opponent; a goal may be scored directly off the kick

Dribbling: advancing the ball with a series of short kicks or taps

Drop ball: when the referee drops the ball between two opponents who each attempt to kick it to a teammate; the soccer equivalent of a jump ball in basketball

Feinting: using deceptive moves, usually of the head and shoulders, to put an opponent off balance

Formation: the way a coach positions the players on a team; a 4–3–3 formation means using four fullbacks, three midfielders and three forwards

Forward: also known as winger, striker and center forward; a player whose primary job is to score goals

Fullback: a player whose primary job is to keep an opponent from scoring or shooting on goal

Goal kick: a kick awarded to a defending team when the attacking team last touched the ball before it went over the endline

Hand ball: the illegal use of the hand or arm by a player

Heading: the use of the forehead to pass or shoot the ball

Indirect free kick: a kick awarded to a team because of a minor foul committed by its opponent; a goal cannot be scored on the kick unless the ball is touched by a player other than the kicker

Linespeople: officials who assist the referee

Marking: guarding an opponent

Midfielder: also known as a halfback; a player who mostly patrols the middle of the field, midfielders are the link between the forwards and the fullbacks

Offside: the referee may rule a player offside when he or she is ahead of the ball in the attacking zone with fewer than two defenders between the player and the goal; the rule does not apply to situations involving free kicks, throw-ins or drop balls

Open space: an area on the field that is not occupied by any players

Penalty kick: a kick awarded to an attacking team when the defending team commits a major violation in the penalty area

Pitch: the traditional name for a soccer field

Punt: when a goalie kicks the ball out of his hands

Referee: the official in charge of a soccer game

Tackling: the technique for taking the ball away from an opponent using the foot or shoulder; tackling is the only situation in soccer in which deliberate body contact is permitted

Throw-in: awarded to a team whose opponent last touched the ball before the ball went over the sideline

Wall: a human barrier of at least three players created to provide assistance to a goalie defending against free kicks

About the Author

Richard Brenner is the author of many sports books for young adults, among them The World Series: The Great Contests, The Complete Super Bowl Story Games I–XXIV, Pro Football's All-Time All-Star Team *and three dual biographies:* Michael Jordan/Magic Johnson, John Elway/Bernie Kosar *and* Roger Clemens/Darryl Strawberry. *He lives in Syosset, New York, with his wife, Anita and children, Hallie and Jason.*

Photography Credits

Tony Duffy/All-Sport: 76

Jan Collsiöö/All-Sport: 9

John Gichigi/All-Sport: 6

Bruce Bennett: 103

Brian Drake: 70

Thomas Zimmermann/FPG Int'l: 61

David Madison: 83, 92, 113

David Madison/Duomo: 27, 119

Bob Thomas Sports Photography: 15, 21, 43, 49, 53, 56, 59, 73, 89, 97, 107

Interior design by Bernard Springsteel
Illustrations by Stanford Kay-Paragraphics